ROSTAM
THE INVINCIBLE

Original story by Ferdowsi
Retold by Jon Mayhew
Series Advisor Professor Kimberley Reynolds
Illustrated by Adrian Stone

OXFORD
UNIVERSITY PRESS

Letter from the Author

I've always loved myths and legends.
One of my earliest memories is of
my father telling me the story of the
Lambton Worm, a dragon story from
the north-east of England. He didn't
read it to me, he just told it and I
listened, trembling with excitement.
From then on, I was hooked.

When I was much, much older, I heard another
storyteller retell the tale of Rostam and, once again, I
was entranced. I wanted to find out more about this
amazing hero.

The tale of Rostam is just a small part of an epic
poem called the *Shahnameh*, or 'Book of Kings', written
by Ferdowsi. He was a poet who was born in the 10th
century, in what is now Iran. His epic poem tells the
story of Persia and the Persian Empire, and is 50 000
verses long. There are many tales in the *Shahnameh* but,
for me, Rostam's adventures are the best.

Jon Mayhew

1. The Simorgh

I am the Simorgh – part eagle, part lion, part dog – mighty ruler of the mountains that tower over the Empire of Persia. Sometimes I show the face of a woman, sometimes that of a fierce animal. These events happened many centuries ago, in a time of myth and legend, before the spread of the Roman Empire, before the conquests of Alexander the Great. This is a story of heroes and villains, of dragons and monsters, of laughter and tragedy.

I used never to get involved with the business of mankind, but that changed many centuries ago when I found a baby, Zal, abandoned on the side of my mountain. Zal's father, Saum, had ordered that he was to be left in the cold and snow. Saum's cruelty towards his son was prompted by the fact that Zal had been born with long white hair – which his father considered the worst of all possible omens.

But baby Zal was strong, like his father, and the cold didn't bother him. I took pity on the poor child and took him back to my nest, where I brought him up with my other young. As the years passed, he continued to grow in strength and eventually became a great hero. He was reunited with his father and together they fought for King Kavus of Persia.

The mightiest and strongest hero of them all, however, was Rostam, the son of Zal. Rostam was a giant of a man, the firmest friend, the fiercest enemy and the most loyal subject a king could wish for. Rostam was stronger than anyone in Persia: he could carry an elephant and crush rocks with his bare hands. Just as I had cared for his father, I watched Rostam grow quickly from a child to a mighty warrior. Rostam loved King Kavus and, along with Zal, tried to advise him whenever he could – but when a monarch is full of pride, he will not always listen. That can lead to his downfall ...

These stories are about Rostam and the amazing feats of courage and endurance he undertook in the King's service, earning for himself the timeless reputation of a hero.

2. Elephant

The whole building shook, making the water jugs rattle together. Rostam blinked and sighed. He rolled over, yawning and stretching, slowly emerging from a deep sleep and a wonderful dream. For a second, he wondered where he was ... and then remembered that he had been sent to meet the King and was sleeping in one of the many guest rooms in the royal palace. Another tremor rumbled through the floor.

'What is that noise?' he called to the guards outside, but there was no reply. The walls shuddered again and a small shower of dust fell from the ceiling on to Rostam's head, making him blink and splutter.

Rubbing his eyes, Rostam staggered over to his bedroom door. He could hear yelling outside now and the loud trumpeting of an elephant. He pulled open the wooden door to his room. In the corridor, two guards stood staring out through the window and didn't notice Rostam appearing from his room.

'What's going on?' said Rostam, frowning at the men.

The two guards jumped away from the window; one squeaked with fright and slammed the shutters closed. The ground thundered now as if there were an earthquake.

'Forgive us, my lord,' the first guard said, bowing. 'We did not hear you enter.'

The other guard stared wide-eyed at Rostam. 'The King's mightiest war elephant is on the loose. It's charging around the courtyard. Three men have been crushed by it already.'

The Great White Elephant belonged to the King, and it was his mightiest war engine. He rode it into battle, to impress and subjugate his enemies. It was twice as big as a normal elephant and had killed many men in war. Rostam could imagine it stamping around outside, trampling the men who had tried to stop it.

'Let me pass! I will stop the beast from killing anyone else!' Rostam said, taking a step towards the door.

The guards looked even more alarmed. 'My lord, please, no,' the first one begged. 'You are only ten years old, and although you are the size of a man already, you are still a child. If anything happened to you, we would lose our heads!'

'So, we just let it stamp around out there until it kills all the King's men, and perhaps the King himself?' Rostam asked scornfully.

The two guards looked at each other and shook their heads. 'I'm sorry, my lord, we can't let you go outside,' they said, folding their arms and blocking the door.

Rostam looked at them. They were tall, strong and fully armed. These were two of his father's best men. That's why Zal had sent them to guard Rostam, his most precious treasure.

'Then I'm sorry too!' Rostam said, and charged at them. The two men, afraid of harming the son of a prince, leaped aside and before they could recover, Rostam charged at the door, kicking it flat to the ground.

The chill night air hit Rostam, making him shiver. The scene outside was one of total chaos. Injured men were lying on the ground, carts rested on their sides where they had been overturned and a small fire had consumed a pile of hay bales in the corner of the courtyard. There, emitting a low, rumbling growl, prowled the elephant. Its colossal body seemed to dominate the whole space. The fire flickered in its eyes as it swung its head, knocking down a poor soldier with its silver-tipped tusks and sending him skidding into the darkness. Other people – servants, stable hands and soldiers – yelled and scurried around the edge of the courtyard, not sure what to do, but desperate to avoid taking on the massive beast that clumped around the cramped space.

Without pausing, the elephant turned and rammed its broad forehead against the walls of the guests' sleeping quarters. A huge crack splintered across the white rendering, exposing mud, brick and straw.

'Hey! Elephant!' Rostam bellowed, striding up to the enormous creature and waving his arms. 'Why don't you go back to bed? You're giving me a headache!'

The elephant lowered its head and butted Rostam, sending him hurtling across the courtyard and thudding against a brick wall. Stars exploded in front of Rostam's eyes and the world spiralled around him. He staggered to his feet and shook himself. Once again, the elephant smashed its head against the walls of the house, bringing down a shower of clay roof tiles and plaster.

'Young master, get away – it's not safe—' a servant began to say, but a sharp smack from the elephant's trunk knocked him unconscious.

Other men began to run away, scrambling up ladders on to the walls of the palace or out through the gateway.

Anger burned in Rostam's belly and he clenched his teeth. 'Very well,' he said, stretching his muscular arms and legs. 'You asked for it.' Rostam ran at the elephant, and, for a moment, it looked confused. Everyone else was running away, but this man – or boy? – was running towards it.

The creature raised its huge foot and slammed it down on Rostam. With a grunt of anger, Rostam grabbed the foot and pushed back with all his might.

The elephant gave a startled trumpet and fell on to its back, rolling and crushing a stack of barrels.

Before the elephant could get to its feet, Rostam grabbed its tusks and swung it round. Servants and soldiers watched in amazement as the elephant spun in a tight circle above Rostam's head. How was it possible? They had heard that Zal's son was unusually large and strong for his age, but they had never imagined him to be so powerful. Rostam grinned as the courtyard whirled around him. The creature's eyes burned with hatred.

'You want me to let you go?' Rostam said. 'As you wish!'

The elephant sailed high over the palace wall and crashed to the ground outside. Rostam ran out through the gate, ready for the next round, but the elephant lay on the earth, out cold.

Rostam dusted his hands clean and then a mighty yawn took him. 'All this excitement in the middle of the night isn't good for a young boy,' he said. 'I need my sleep.' And he strode back into the palace and returned to his bedroom, where the two guards stood frozen in amazement. Rostam grinned at them and climbed back into his bed. Soon he was snoring louder than any elephant.

News of Rostam's adventure with the elephant spread
through the palace and quickly reached the King's ears. I,
the Simorgh, watched from afar as news of Rostam's great
strength and power spread across the land. Rostam was
proclaimed a hero and a future saviour of Persia.

When Zal heard the news he was proud of Rostam, but
troubled too, because although his son was still young, it
seemed the cares of the world were about to catch up with
him. Zal would have liked him to spend a little longer as a
child, but Persia wanted a hero.

'And a hero must have a horse,' Zal said to himself. 'As
soon as my son returns home, we shall find him a stallion
worthy of a mighty warrior.'

3. Lightning Horse

Herds of horses stamped and swirled around the courtyard of Zal's grand fortress, kicking up the dust into a fog. Rostam watched from the marble steps as the herdsmen whistled and coaxed the horses around, parading in front of him.

Zal put a hand on Rostam's arm. 'It's time for you to choose a horse,' Zal said. 'For even though you are still a child, you tower above all of us and, in time, you will be a warrior like no other!'

Rostam grinned down at Zal. His father spoke the truth. Even now, Rostam could arm-wrestle all of Zal's strongest bodyguards until they begged him to release his iron grip. 'You do me a great honour, Father,' he said, bowing to Zal. 'Which shall I choose?'

'It will have to be a horse that can match your strength, Rostam, my son,' Zal said, proudly. 'Go down there and try some out.'

One of the herdsmen, wrapped in a ragged robe and turban, led Rostam down into the courtyard. Rostam's heart thumped as the horses around him jostled each other and skittered out of his way when he reached for them. He could see tails and rumps and legs and manes and wild eyes staring at him. Snorts, whinnies and the thunder of hooves filled his ears.

'What are these marks on the horses' rumps?' he asked the herdsman.

'Those are the brands to show who owns which horse,' the herdsman replied, grinning. 'Your father will pay the owner of your chosen horse handsomely!'

Rostam frowned at the horses as they trotted around him, weaving in and out of the herd while the herdsmen clicked their tongues and cracked their whips. *Which one to choose?* he wondered. *Maybe a midnight black stallion?*

He reached out and tangled his fingers in a passing stallion's mane. It jerked to a halt and fell to the ground with a whinny of surprise.

The herdsman ran forward. 'My lord Rostam, you need to be gentle,' he said, bowing slightly and coaxing the horse back to its feet. 'You have the strength of ten men and could so easily drag any mount to the ground.'

Rostam felt his cheeks redden. He ran a hand softly along the stallion's neck. 'Forgive me, fine creature. I didn't mean to harm you.' The horse calmed down but Rostam shook his head. 'This is too delicate a mount for me – I fear its legs would buckle under my weight.'

A grey with a long flying mane cantered past and Rostam pointed to it. The herdsman caught the horse and brought it to Rostam. The horse grunted as the huge boy settled himself on its back. Rostam felt the creature's whole body tremble, then the tremble became a shudder and the horse slumped to the ground, leaving him standing astride its panting body.

'Maybe not that one, either, sire,' the herdsman said with a shrug.

A chestnut mare caught Rostam's eye and they brought it to him, but when he grabbed the saddle to pull himself up, he dragged the poor horse to the ground. 'Some days, it isn't good to be so strong,' he muttered under his breath.

Rostam tried one horse after another, but each one crumpled under his weight, or went tumbling into a corner of the courtyard whenever he pulled on the reins a little too hard. Hissing with frustration, he stormed out of the courtyard to a nearby field. There, he saw a grey mare and a young stallion. One of the herdsmen ran to follow him.

Rostam held his breath. The stallion was three years old, at the peak of fitness, and its hide shone like copper in the sunset. Its long black mane blew in the wind like a war flag. 'Whose horse is that?' he breathed.

The herdsman fidgeted. 'Oh, him, sire? He's nobody's horse,' he said. 'Best to just leave him alone.'

Rostam grinned. 'Just the words I wanted to hear,' he said. 'Why is it best to leave him?'

The herdsman's eyes widened. 'It's not him,' he said. 'It's his mother, the grey mare. She is so protective of him. Many a nobleman has sworn to ride that stallion only to be mauled by the mare.'

At that moment, Rostam knew that he would ride the stallion. His heart thumped against his ribs and he clenched his fists. 'She doesn't scare me,' he said, striding towards the pair of horses.

The grey mare looked up from grazing as Rostam marched forward, but Rostam felt his strength pulse through every muscle. *Nothing will stop me.* The mare pawed the ground and snorted.

But I don't want to harm an innocent animal, he thought. *There's no honour in that. She's a mother protecting her young one.*

The mare's walk became a trot which turned into a canter and then a full gallop. She neighed and tossed her head, flinging her huge hooves forward.

Rostam sidestepped the attack and just as the mare turned, he drew a deep breath, filling his enormous lungs with air. Then he let out a mighty roar. The mare skidded to a halt, blinking, her hooves scraping the dirt as she slid towards Rostam. Then she turned on her hind legs and fled.

With a smile, Rostam walked over to the stallion. He unhooked his rope from his belt and made a lasso. With perfect aim, he got the rope around the horse's neck first time. The horse pulled at the rope but Rostam didn't let go. 'He's strong!' Rostam yelled. 'Bring me a saddle!'

The herdsman ran over to Rostam with a saddle and a bridle.

Rostam pulled on the rope, but the horse dug his hooves into the dirt. With a smile of satisfaction, the boy realized that the animal was his equal in strength. 'Now *this* is the mount for me!' he muttered, working his way hand-over-hand along the rope towards the horse. The herdsman followed, the saddle shaking in his hands.

Finally, Rostam reached the horse's head and put out a gentle hand. The horse nuzzled Rostam and let the boy stroke his neck.

'He's a fine animal, sire,' the herdsman said. The horse snorted as if to say, *And what would you know about it?*

'Rakhsh!' Rostam whispered.

'Pardon, my lord?' the herdsman said.

'His name is Rakhsh!' Rostam said, putting his arms around the stallion's neck. 'After the lightning that flashes in the sky. Give me the saddle!'

Soon Rostam had secured the saddle and climbed up. Rakhsh stood firm and Rostam kicked him forward. The stallion walked easily with Rostam's huge frame on his back. Boy and horse moved as if they had been made for each other.

'A fine and fearsome mount,' the herdsman said, panting as he ran alongside them. Rostam grinned and was about to kick Rakhsh on, but the horse seemed to read his mind and broke into a fierce gallop. The air thundered with the sound of Rakhsh's hooves and Rostam whooped and cheered as he charged through the fields. He was ready for adventure!

And that is how Rostam met Rakhsh. They were firm friends from that point onwards, but soon both rider and trusty mount would be called upon to face great perils and seemingly impossible challenges. However, for Rostam and Rakhsh, nothing was impossible.

The bond between Rostam and Rakhsh strengthened and they were rarely apart. As a child, Rostam stood head and shoulders above most of the men in the King's guard but, as he grew older, he grew taller still and became a giant amongst men. Rakhsh grew in pace with his master, and the pair were a fearsome sight on any battlefield.

Nobody doubted Rostam's bravery, but there is a difference between a brave soldier and a hero. A true hero faces many challenges with good grace. The Greek hero Hercules was set twelve tasks or labours and performed them with an ill will. Rostam, however, willingly accepted his trials, even if he faced them only because of the foolishness of his King, as the next story will show.

4. The Greedy King

King Kavus sat in his garden, surrounded by bodyguards, servants and ladies-in-waiting. He lay in the shade of a rose-covered bower, drinking from a crystal goblet. Around him, his noblemen, dressed in rich silks, discussed the latest conquests his armies had made and bragged about the gold and silver they had brought to his palace from the cities that trembled at his might. Kavus smiled. Everything was good. He had more than he needed; his people worshipped and obeyed him. They feared him, too, which was best of all.

'Nobody is greater than you, sire,' one general said. 'Your empire stretches beyond the horizon and has no compare.'

Kavus smiled, picked a ruby the size of a tomato from a pile of jewels and tossed it to the general. 'Well said,' Kavus replied, smiling. The general smiled back and bowed deeply.

Before he could say any more, a wide-eyed and trembling servant shuffled before Kavus and threw himself on the floor in front of him. 'Forgive the intrusion of a humble slave, oh mighty one,' the servant said, his voice quivering, 'but a wandering minstrel is outside the palace and begs the chance to sing you one song.'

Kavus stared down at the shivering messenger. 'Is he any good?' he demanded.

The servant's eyes widened even more. 'His voice sounds sweet and he plays the lute exquisitely,' he said, casting his eyes down once more. 'But I am a mere slave, Your Greatness. Only you have the taste and wisdom to judge ... '

Kavus laughed and waved a hand at the servant. 'Send this minstrel in. We shall hear his song.'

The minstrel was ushered into the garden and everyone gasped. Nobody had ever seen such a handsome man. He stood tall even over the fiercest of the King's warriors and yet he was lithe and slender. His long black hair was swept back to reveal an almond-shaped face and laughing blue eyes. Kavus frowned. *This man is better-looking than me!* he thought. *That's not right.* Just looking at this minstrel made Kavus feel discontented and jealous.

The minstrel bowed smoothly. 'Your Majesty,' he said. 'Thank you for honouring me with a chance to sing for you.' Even the man's voice sounded rich and musical!

Kavus coughed uncomfortably, trying to crush the dislike he felt. 'You are most welcome, minstrel. What are you going to sing for us?'

The minstrel's face clouded slightly, making some of the ladies-in-waiting sigh with pity. 'A song about my home country, Your Highness,' he said. 'A country that I miss. The land of Mazanderan!'

The party gasped. They had all heard of Mazanderan, a beautiful land but one with a dark reputation.

The minstrel began to sing. Despite himself, Kavus felt bewitched by the music. The minstrel described his homeland and its forests, where hunting was plentiful and flowers bloomed in their thousands. The honey from the bees that flew amongst those flowers was the most delectable any man had tasted. The minstrel described jewelled castles, rich farmland, rivers glistening with fish. A land where it is always spring and never winter.

As Kavus listened, his envy of the man and his home country grew. A thought wormed its way into his head and then burrowed deep in his heart. *I should be king of this land*, he thought. *I will invade it, subdue its people and take it for myself.*

The minstrel finished his song and the party burst into applause without waiting for the King to lead them. But Kavus's mind was on other things: he could see himself receiving tribute from this rich land – piles of gold, heaps of silver, the finest food and drink. It would all be his.

'My lord?' a noble said, his voice sounding worried. King Kavus shook himself. He'd been deep in thought and hadn't noticed that the clapping had stopped. The minstrel stood, head bowed, awaiting a response from the King.

'Forgive me,' King Kavus said. 'Your song enchanted me, minstrel. Here.' He gave the minstrel an emerald the size of an apple.

The minstrel took the jewel and bowed deeply. 'Your Majesty does me a great honour.' And, with a last smile for the King, he retreated from the garden.

Kavus couldn't help thinking that the minstrel was mocking him. He thought about sending guards to have the minstrel thrown into prison. *But no,* he thought, *when I am King of Mazanderan, he will play for me until his fingers bleed and his voice dries out to a raven's croak.*

When the minstrel had vanished from sight, Kavus clapped his hands, dismissing the servants. 'Come, my generals,' he said. 'While we sit here, idle, our enemies plot against us. We must plan our next conquest.'

The generals looked at each other in confusion. 'But where, my lord?' they said. 'Your empire stretches as far as the eye can see. What lands are left to conquer?'

'Mazanderan!' King Kavus said, smacking his fist into his palm. 'Such a land of wonders and wealth should be under my control.'

The generals looked dismayed. 'But, Your Highness,' one man said, 'the King of Mazanderan has powerful allies. Everyone knows that the country is protected by the mighty White Devourer!'

Everyone but the King shivered at the mention of the name. They knew stories of the monster that dwelt in Mazanderan. It was said that whole armies had vanished into Mazanderan, never to return. Once, a powerful bandit chief had led his men into the country to rob and pillage. His men were never seen again but the chief staggered back across the border, blind and weeping like a lost child.

'I am King Kavus,' the King snapped, breaking the silence and making everyone jump. 'Who is more powerful than I? Are we to hide in fear of some mythical creature? No! Mazanderan will bow down to me or I will burn it to the ground. Now go and make plans for invasion!'

The generals didn't move. They stared at the ground in shame. 'We are your willing slaves, oh mighty one, and will do whatever you ask of us,' they said. 'But our love for you compels us to point out that no king of Persia has dared to invade Mazanderan, ever.'

'Then I will be the first,' Kavus said. 'And the last.'

The generals watched as Kavus swept out of the garden. 'You may indeed be the first king of Persia to invade Mazanderan, my lord,' one of them muttered, 'but as for the last – I fear it is more likely to be the last thing you do.'

5. A Cry for Help

About a month later, Rostam stood outside the stables running a brush through Rakhsh's thick mane. He could have asked a servant to do it but they were always so terrified that the stallion might kill them. Also, not many of the servants could actually reach the top of the horse's neck without standing on a barrel. Anyway, he loved the smell of horses, and Rakhsh was his best friend. Rostam felt himself calming down as the heavy bristles swished through the hair. Rakhsh breathed a snorting sigh, enjoying the moment of peace. Then he pricked his ears up and glanced around the stable yard.

Rostam frowned. 'What is it, boy?' he said. 'Do we have company?' He glanced round and saw his father Zal striding over, his hair shining white in the sunlight.

'My father,' Rostam said, bowing. 'What can I do for you?'

Zal looked troubled. Deep lines furrowed his pale brow. 'There's a problem,' Zal said.

Rostam dropped his brush and puffed out his chest. 'Then tell me what it is, my lord, and I shall deal with it immediately.'

Zal held up a calming hand. 'Enough, Rostam. I will tell you, but too much eagerness will get you into trouble, as it has our King, I fear. As you know, the King left for Mazanderan over a month ago, but instead of a cheerful messenger bringing news of victory, a lone soldier has just appeared at the palace, slumped over the neck of his horse.'

'One soldier?' Rostam said. 'What has happened to the King and his army?'

'It's well known that the King of Mazanderan is protected by the White Devourer, a powerful and terrifying creature,' Zal said. 'The soldier told us that it sent a huge cloud of darkness over Kavus's army. Half of the King's men were overcome with fear and turned against Kavus himself, so that the other half of the army had to defend him. Then the cloud that the Devourer had sent poisoned the surviving men and robbed them of their sight. The poor soldiers were left wandering the battlefield, blind and terrified.'

Rostam felt flames of anger burning in his heart.

'A cowardly way to fight,' murmured Rostam.

Zal nodded. 'Now the King and what is left of his men sit huddled in a dark dungeon,' he said. 'The White Devourer has ordered that they shall not be killed but will be left there to suffer.'

'I must save them,' Rostam said, through gritted teeth.

'I fear you are the only one who can rescue the King and his army, Rostam,' Zal said, 'but you must be careful. There is no place for pride when you face creatures of darkness. They rely on you thinking you can win easily. It is not my place to criticize the King, but this was the weakness that caused his downfall.'

'How do I get to Mazanderan?' Rostam said, stroking Rakhsh's neck.

'There are two main routes,' Zal replied. 'One is the route the King took. It is long, and even if you were to ride Rakhsh as fast as the wind, with no time to stop and rest, it would take you weeks.'

'The King can't last that long,' Rostam said.

Rakhsh snorted and stamped his feet as if to say, *What are we waiting for? Let's go!*

'The second route is full of danger,' Zal said. 'Monsters, wild beasts and bandits haunt every inch of the path. Those who choose this path rarely come out alive, but it is the shorter of the two.'

'I must take the shorter route,' Rostam declared. 'I will prepare supplies and leave today.' He clasped his father's shoulder. 'Fear not. We will save the King!'

Rostam rode into the wilderness that very day, eager to rescue the King. Nobody doubted his bravery but, in this strange and punishing land, even Rostam's incredible strength and his quick wits would be put to the test. Fortunately, he took Rakhsh with him ...

6. Night Stalker

Rostam rode through pleasant woodland and listened to the birds singing in the shady canopy of leaves. 'This doesn't seem so bad,' he said to Rakhsh, who snorted in agreement.

Soon, however, the trees grew shorter and the leaves grew thinner. The ground became harder and the sun beat down on Rostam's head. He gulped from his waterskin and wiped the sweat from his brow. All day they travelled towards the distant horizon that wobbled in the heat haze. Vultures circled overhead, their forlorn cries echoing high above him.

By night time, exhaustion weighed heavily on Rostam. The sun disappeared, leaving a cold, cloudless sky. Icy stars shone down. Rostam lit a fire and then, cocooned in his blanket, fell into a deep, dreamless sleep.

Rakhsh rolled his eyes and shook his head at the snoring hero. *Don't mind me, I'll just find myself something to eat,* he thought, and began searching for any blade of grass he could nibble at. The dusty ground held no surprises apart from a nose full of sand that made Rakhsh snort and sneeze. He pawed the dry earth with his hoof, but found nothing.

Nearby was a spiny thorn bush with some tiny leaves and Rakhsh decided that these would have to do.

The thorns didn't really trouble him as they might other horses. The vultures had gone away for now; that was one thing to be grateful for. Rakhsh couldn't stand their horrible screeching. At least it was quiet now. *Too quiet,* Rakhsh suddenly thought, glancing around.

A sudden movement made Rakhsh wheel round and jump back. A lion leaped up at him from the darkness, catching him by surprise. With a roar, the lion slashed at Rakhsh with its claws.

Rakhsh skipped back easily and flicked out a front hoof. It caught the lion square in the jaw and sent it wheeling across the smouldering remains of Rostam's fire. The hero himself snored on.

Recovering itself, the lion pounced again, but Rakhsh spun round and lashed out with both rear hooves. This time there was a crunch of bone as the lion screeched with agony and rage. Rakhsh turned on the lion again and sunk his teeth into the fierce creature, shaking it and slamming it down on the ground. Then the lion lay still.

Rakhsh stood, panting over the fallen beast, recovering from the battle. He felt sorry for the creature, but it would have eaten him if he hadn't fought back. Behind him, Rakhsh heard another rumbling growl and spun round, ready to face a new attack. Then he heaved a sigh of relief. The noise was nothing more than his master lying on his back, snoring so hard Rakhsh thought he might blow the moon off course.

Rostam awoke and stretched in the cold, grey light of dawn. The fire was cold and a light dew coated his blanket. He shivered and looked around for Rakhsh. 'Morning, horse,' he said, with a yawn. 'I had the strangest dream last night … ' Rostam stopped and stared at the dead lion. 'You defeated this huge beast alone?' he said in wonder. Then he shook his head. 'I thought you were a clever horse! You should have woken me. What if this lion had eaten you? I would have had to walk to Mazanderan! Next time, wake me up!'

Rakhsh rolled his eyes and shook himself. Sometimes it was hard being a hero's horse.

So Rostam had faced his first challenge without even waking up! But sometimes danger doesn't spring from the shadows. It glares down at you from the sky and no amount of armour, or even a mighty stallion, can protect you.

7. Desert Heat

The day began brightly and Rostam felt well rested after a good night's sleep. He whistled as he rode along, and it seemed as though Rakhsh nodded in time. As the sun climbed higher in the sky, however, Rostam became less tuneful. The heat made his armour unbearable to wear and he hung it over Rakhsh's saddlebags. By late morning, Rostam had drained the last of the water from his waterskin and dismounted. It seemed unfair to ride Rakhsh in this heat: the poor horse placed one hoof in front of the other as if each had been weighed down with lead.

The ground became smoother and more silken; hot sand buried any rocks that might have once poked out. Rostam panted as he trudged alongside Rakhsh, and his head throbbed. His tongue felt fifteen times its normal size inside his mouth. He tried to lick his cracked lips but didn't have the spit to do it.

'We need to find water,' he said to Rakhsh, who nodded.

The sweat on Rostam's burning skin evaporated, leaving stinging salt. Eventually, he became too dried out even to sweat.

The vultures circled overhead and Rostam shook a feeble fist at them. 'You're not getting us,' he croaked. 'Go and look for food somewhere else!'

Many times in his short life, Rostam had been faced with challenges, but they were usually ones he could fight or puzzle his way out of. This challenge was one of pure endurance, a simple act of ignoring the heat and moving forwards.

Rostam's throat burned with every breath and his muscles ached as he trudged through the scalding sand. He stopped and frowned at the horizon, squinting through crusted eyelashes. It seemed to shimmer, and then, just below it, a lake of silver water appeared.

'Water,' he whispered, quickening his pace. 'Water, Rakhsh! We're saved!'

Half-running, half-stumbling, Rostam dragged himself towards the shining lake of water while Rakhsh limped along behind him, whinnying gently – but no matter how fast Rostam ran, the water always seemed just out of reach.

Finally, gasping for breath, he fell on to the burning sand.

'A mirage,' Rostam panted. He'd been told about these shimmering patches caused by the sun reflecting off the heat haze. Those desperate with thirst often mistook them for water.

'This was a fool's errand, that's for sure,' he croaked, banging his fist on the hot ground. 'Whose idea was it to go wandering in the desert?'

Rakhsh gave another faint whinny and shook his head. *Not mine!* he thought, and nodded his head again. *Anyway, stop moaning and use your eyes.*

Rostam frowned at the horizon again. 'Could it be?' he said. There in the distance, green palm leaves nodded in a faint breeze. 'Trees!' Rostam shouted. 'And where there are trees, there is water!' He tried to clamber to his feet but his knees buckled beneath him and he fell heavily back to the ground. Gritting his teeth, Rostam pushed himself up, only to fall again. He lay gasping for breath. To be so close to water and safety, and yet not have the strength to walk!

A shadow crossed Rostam's gaze as Rakhsh lowered himself on to the sand and gave Rostam a nudge with his nose. Rostam gripped the saddle and pulled himself across Rakhsh's back. When Rakhsh stood up, Rostam hung over him like a sack of corn, but he didn't care. This was no time for pride.

His legs wobbling with exhaustion and his master's dead weight, Rakhsh slowly stumbled through the sand.

After a while, a cool refreshing breeze blew across Rostam's face, and gradually he forced his eyes open. Rakhsh lowered himself down so that his master slid off on to the bank of a large oasis. Birds waded in the water and skimmed across its surface. Tall palm trees shaded Rostam and Rakhsh from the glare of the sun. Slowly, Rostam slid a burning hand into the cold water and scooped out a mouthful. Then he trickled a little on to his scalded lips, letting it soothe and revive him.

He splashed more water on to his face and gasped as it chilled his blistered skin. Then he plunged his head totally under the surface and drank in a whole mouthful of water. Rakhsh drank slowly and carefully beside him, and watched as Rostam came back from the dead.

They spent the rest of the day recovering from their ordeal in the desert. Rostam found some fruit and managed to trap some birds and roast them over a fire. As evening fell, he yawned and stretched.

'Well, Rakhsh, you saved my life and for that I am forever grateful,' he said, patting the horse. 'But now I am tired and will sleep. Tomorrow, we will continue our journey to rescue the King!'

Praise indeed! Rakhsh thought, but he nuzzled his master, glad that he was alive and well.

Rostam wrapped his blanket around himself and curled up by the fire to sleep. It wasn't to be the most peaceful night, however, as something lurked in the shadows of the oasis and watched them with a hungry gaze …

8. Claws and Fangs of Shadow

Once again, Rostam's mighty snoring shook the night. Rakhsh tried to ignore the tiresome noise that vibrated through his hooves and up his fetlocks. The day had been long and he was tired, too.

Rakhsh lowered his head and wondered if he should rest for a moment, but the encounter with the lion the night before had left him on edge. *If danger comes calling, I want to be awake to alert the master. I don't want him to be cross, like he was when I killed that lion.* Rakhsh lowered himself to the ground and rolled in the dust. *I'll just settle here and rest my legs,* he thought. *I won't go to sleep, though.*

Despite Rostam's cacophonous snoring and the possibility of danger, Rakhsh's eyelids began to droop. *Maybe I should stand up*, he thought, but it felt so nice to be lying on the warm sand that he stayed where he was.

Something slid through the water, making the tiniest splash. Rakhsh leaped up and slammed his hooves down on to the ground. Immediately, Rostam threw off his blanket and drew his sword.

'What is it, Rakhsh? Trouble?' he said, searching the shadows for any threat.

Rakhsh glared into the waters of the oasis. *I could've*

sworn there was something there, he thought.

Rostam sheathed his sword and pulled his blanket around him. 'Dozy horse,' he muttered. 'Afraid of his own shadow … ' Soon he was snoring once more.

Rakhsh blew out an indignant breath. *Dozy?* he thought. *I'll show him!* Throwing his head up, he sniffed the air. Something didn't smell quite right, he was certain. The reflection of the night sky wobbled on the surface of the water. A sinewy shape twisted and turned just beneath it. Clawed fingers broke the surface with a plop, and a red eye blinked at Rakhsh.

With a neigh of alarm, Rakhsh reared up and brought his iron hooves down on the ground once again.

And once again, Rostam was on his feet, his sword in hand. 'Trouble, Rakhsh?' he bellowed, scanning the darkness for any sign of a threat – but whatever Rakhsh had seen had sunk without a trace.

It was there! I saw it! Rakhsh thought, pawing the ground with his hoof and trying to make Rostam understand.

'Curse you, Rakhsh! What are you trying to do?' Rostam growled, driving his sword deep into the sand. 'If you wake me up again, I swear I'll leave you tied up at this oasis and carry all my armour and weapons across the desert myself.'

Humph! Rakhsh thought. *I'd like to see you do that!*

Grumbling and muttering, Rostam threw himself down again, flapping his blanket and dragging it around his huge body. The grumbling soon became a growling snore, as loud as a hibernating bear in a cave.

Again, Rakhsh stood alone, frowning into the depths of the water. *I probably couldn't sleep with all that noise anyway,* he thought, glancing over at the rumbling mountain of man and blanket. *And I definitely saw something out there.*

The night grew colder and Rakhsh shivered a little, puffing breath out through his flaring nostrils. He knew Rostam wouldn't really leave him behind; he was just full of bluster. Rakhsh gave a little whinny of amusement as he imagined his master grunting and staggering through the desert laden with armour, weapons and saddlebags.

Another splash shattered his reverie. The water of the oasis roiled and seethed as a massive, scaly head rose out of it, lifted by a long, snake-like body. The creature's eyes blazed and it grinned with a mouth full of needle-sharp teeth.

Rakhsh didn't even think about Rostam's earlier warning, but gave an ear-splitting neigh and pounded the earth until Rostam leaped up, thinking there was an earthquake.

'What have I told you about ... ' Rostam began to say, but the sight of the enormous serpent rising from the lake stole the words from his mouth. Its sinewy body swayed above him, black scales glistening wet in the starlight. Four pairs of long arms sprouted from its sides, each arm ending in four clawed fingers.

'Tell me your name, hero,' the serpent hissed, its crimson eyes

boring into Rostam's. 'I like to know whose bones I am about to feast upon.'

'I am Rostam, son of Zal, and I'm not afraid of you!' Rostam roared, beating his chest with his fist. 'Go back into your lake, serpent, or I will use your skin as an umbrella to shade me in the desert sun!'

'Your mother will weep for your death, Rostam,' the serpent said, giving a wicked chuckle, 'but she will never know where your body lies.'

'Are you going to stand there all night and try to kill me with words?' Rostam snorted. 'Come and fight. I want to get this over with so I can go back to sleep!'

With a hiss of rage the serpent darted forward, its long body uncoiling from the water. Snatching up his sword from where he had planted it in the sand earlier, Rostam leaped at the serpent and chopped at the creature's body. But the huge reptile swirled around Rostam, easily dodging the blow and wrapping the warrior's chest in its strong coils.

Rostam felt the creature start to crush his ribs and he braced himself, dropping his sword and gripping the scaly coils tight. He squeezed the serpent's body in his hands, crushing it just as it tried to crush him. Rakhsh leaped forward and with his front hooves landed a powerful blow to the monster's head.

Dazed, the serpent released Rostam, who grabbed hold of its tail and began to swing it around his head. Just as the serpent's head reached Rakhsh's hind legs, he kicked out. The serpent went sailing across the oasis, powered by Rakhsh's mighty kick, and landed with a thump that shook the earth.

For a second all was silent, then Rostam looked over at Rakhsh, who snorted and pawed the ground. Rostam's laughter echoed over the oasis.

'Some monster, eh, Rakhsh?' Rostam said, striding over to the horse and patting his neck. Rakhsh neighed in agreement.

The trees that surrounded the oasis shuddered and the creature burst from between them. Its eyes blazing with anger, the serpent hissed as it shot towards Rostam and Rakhsh like an arrow. Rostam fell back, pinned by the serpent's claws. It lashed him with its tail, making stars blossom before his eyes. Suddenly, Rostam was face-to-face with the creature, his hands around its neck, trying to push the snapping teeth away from him.

Sweat poured down the hero's face and his huge muscles bulged as he struggled to keep the jaws from biting his face. But Rakhsh sank his teeth into the serpent's shoulder, pulling it away from Rostam.

Rostam's sword glinted in the starlight, abandoned on the ground. He snatched it up and sliced through the serpent's neck, sending its head whirling off into the darkness. Black liquid spilled across the sands. Some of it touched Rostam, burning his bare skin and making him yell in agony.

Without pausing, Rostam leaped into the cold water, gasping and thankful as it washed away the poisonous blood that had sprayed from the serpent's flailing body. Rakhsh followed him, paddling out into the depths and away from danger.

As the acid blood soaked into the sand, they waded back to the shore.

Rostam planted one foot on the serpent's belly and waved his sword in the air. 'I am Rostam!' he bellowed. 'The greatest hero in the land! Not lions, nor serpents, nor even the desert's fearsome heat can overcome me! I am invincible!'

Rakhsh shook his mane and went over to the other side of the oasis to nibble on the sweet grass that grew by the side of the water.

No doubt there'd be more challenges tomorrow.

Once more, Rostam's marvellous horse, Rakhsh, quietly and unassumingly saved the hero's life. And he was right that more challenges lay in wait. Indeed, the next challenge would prove to be one of the strangest ...

9. The Feast from Nowhere

Rostam and Rakhsh left the oasis and ventured deep into the desert again. Rostam had learned his lesson and filled his waterskins until they were fat and heavy.

The sun beat down, searing Rostam's skin. 'I wish I *had* made a parasol out of that serpent back at the oasis, now,' he muttered to Rakhsh as they plodded on. Rakhsh's head hung low and his ears drooped. Rostam gazed across the flat, featureless desert and took another sip from the waterskin. Then, dismounting, he poured some water into Rakhsh's nosebag, passing it to the horse, who drank greedily.

The day wore on and Rostam began to despair of ever getting out of the desert. 'Maybe we've taken a wrong turn, Rakhsh,' he said. 'I should've known better than to follow you blindly!'

Rakhsh gave a snort.

The waterskins grew thin and Rostam panted in the heat. 'Rakhsh, my friend,' he said, 'you'll forgive me if we run out of food and I have to eat you, won't you?'

Rakhsh shook his head. It was too hot for Rostam's silly jokes. They plodded on, and gradually the ground became rocky, and shrubs and coarse grass began to appear. A little while longer and short, scrubby trees dotted the desert. Rakhsh nibbled a few leaves as they passed but they were bitter and salty. But gradually, the land became greener and a deep forest appeared on the skyline.

Rostam craned his neck, standing up in the stirrups and nearly sending the exhausted Rakhsh to his knees. 'I don't believe it,' Rostam muttered. 'It must be another mirage.' He slid out of the saddle, ignoring Rakhsh's sigh of relief, and ran through the scrubby undergrowth.

The trees nearby waved in a gentle breeze, but on the open grassland before them sat a table, covered with a crisp white cloth and laden with food. A jug stood in the middle, and golden plates of fruit, bread and meat surrounded it.

'Luck is on our side, old friend,' Rostam called to Rakhsh. He sat down and began to tear chunks off the bread and bite into the joints of meat. He looked up to see Rakhsh staring at him. 'What?' Rostam said, shrugging. 'What do you want me to do? Leave it?'

Rakhsh gave a low nicker and looked towards the treeline. Were there people watching?

Rostam frowned as he chewed slowly on a crust of soft bread. 'Do you think this might be a trap, Rakhsh?'

Rakhsh gave a snort and nodded his head.

For a moment, Rostam looked thoughtfully over at the trees, and then shrugged again. 'Ah well,' he said. 'If this is poisoned, it's too late now; if it's not, then it's too good to waste!'

Rakhsh watched his master shovel fruit and meat and bread and drink down his hungry throat. After some time, he let out a huge belch that sent birds fluttering from the nearby trees and bushes. 'Delicious!' Rostam declared. He peered again at the treeline. Someone was walking towards him.

Rostam grinned. A beautiful woman, dressed in the finest silks, sauntered across the fields.

'Who do we have here, Rakhsh?' Rostam muttered. 'A good job she didn't hear me belch. That would've been bad manners.'

Rakhsh blew out a long breath, as if to say, *EVERYONE heard you belch.*

The woman reached the table and smiled at Rostam. 'Have you eaten enough, sir?' she asked, tucking a strand of her long black hair behind her ear.

'Yes, thank you,' Rostam said, feeling his cheeks redden. 'Forgive me, but I have travelled through the desert for many hours, and I was hungry.'

She smiled and pulled a chair out next to him. 'No need to apologize,' she said, smiling. 'Stay and have some more.'

Rostam grinned and settled back. 'Why not?' he said, popping a grape into his mouth. 'It's pleasant here, the food is good and the company is wonderful.'

'And you don't have anywhere important to go, do you?' the woman said, smiling with dazzling white teeth.

Rostam's eyes felt heavy. 'No, I don't think so,' he said, his voice slurring.

'You just have to stay here and enjoy the food,' the woman said, her words echoing in his mind.

'Just stay here,' Rostam repeated.

A shadow fell across his face and Rakhsh leaped over the table, clipping it with his huge iron hooves. The jug tipped over, spilling its contents into the woman's lap. Loaves and apples, joints of meat and dates flew everywhere. Rostam tumbled backwards on his chair and stared up in wonder as the woman screeched with rage and drew a strange dagger with a curved blade.

Rakhsh ran to Rostam's side. Suddenly, all Rostam's senses were clear again and alert to the danger. He jumped to his feet and, snatching up the rope that hung on the saddle, he threw it around the woman, snaring her arms in a lasso. Once again she screamed as the rope pulled tight, pinning her arms.

'Who are you?' Rostam demanded, tugging at the rope. 'Why did you try to bewitch me with this food?'

The woman's face twisted into a mask of hatred and anger. Slowly, she began to change. Her hair grew white and straggly, her silken robes became black rags, warts covered her withered skin. She grinned at Rostam through broken, yellowed teeth.

'Darkness shall fall upon you, *hero*, and your way will not be clear,' she muttered, straining at the rope. 'You will wander like a lost sheep in the wilderness until starvation takes you.'

'Enough!' Rostam yelled and yanked on the rope. It tightened around the woman. She gave a final howl of hatred and exploded into flames, leaving nothing but foul-smelling smoke and dust that blew away on the breeze. Rostam stared in disbelief at the slack rope.

'This is a strange land, Rakhsh,' he said. 'I fear that woman may have sent us off course with her words.'

Rostam's fears proved true, but whether the woman had enchanted him or exhaustion took its toll, we'll never know. Sometimes, the biggest challenges come from inside our own minds.

10. Olad

Rostam rode in silence through the forest, wondering about what the woman had said. Her words weighed heavily on him. As if sensing this extra burden, Rakhsh plodded along, his ears back and head low.

The forest grew thicker, the light blotted out by the tangle of branches above. Unknown things whispered and hissed in the shadows between the trees, and spindly branches brushed Rostam's face like dead men's fingers.

'I don't like this place, Rakhsh,' Rostam muttered, batting an overhanging branch out of his way.

The further they travelled, the more intense the darkness became. After several hours of riding, Rostam wasn't certain if they were still in a forest or on an open plain. The black night consumed everything. He lifted his hand in front of his face but could not see it. A deep gloom settled on Rostam's heart. 'What's the point, Rakhsh?' He sighed. 'This darkness sucks any joy from me. I fear we'll never escape it.'

Rakhsh didn't stop walking.

It seemed as if the stars and the moon had been stolen and a black cloth flung across the world. Rostam listened out for any sound: a stream, a bird or even the wind blowing in his ears. Silence reigned in this dark place.

Sometimes he even struggled to hear Rakhsh's feet on the ground.

'Have I lost my senses?' he said, patting Rakhsh for reassurance. He could still feel the horse beneath him. With a sigh, Rostam dropped the reins. 'Go where you want to, Rakhsh, it makes no difference here. Left is as good as right in such pitch blackness, up is as good as down.'

Rostam bowed his head and let his eyes close. For a moment, he thought of getting down and lying on the ground but he couldn't even see it from where he sat, high up on Rakhsh's back. He could have been riding through the dark night sky for all he knew.

At some point, Rostam must have dozed, because he awoke to find it was light and he was slipping sideways. With a yell, he slid off the saddle and found himself face-down in thick golden wheat. Rakhsh had stopped and was eagerly tearing up mouthful after mouthful.

Rostam narrowed his eyes at the horse. 'You greedy beast,' he muttered, dusting himself down. Rakhsh looked up briefly but quickly fell back to eating. Rostam smiled. 'I suppose I looked much the same when I wolfed down the strange woman's feast, eh, Rakhsh?'

Rakhsh snorted without looking up.

The field stretched all around Rostam. Distant mountains shimmered in the heat haze, and a little nearer, trees dotted the landscape. It looked like a rich and fertile land, but Rostam had no idea where he was.

'Hey!' A voice made Rostam jump, and he turned round just in time to be smacked across the face with a stick. Rostam roared and grabbed the stick, snapping it and wrenching it from its owner's hand at the same time.

The owner was a small, ragged man with a dirty face and a straggly beard. His eyes were wide with fear. 'Y–you shouldn't let your h–horse eat my m–master's wh–wheat,' he stammered, realizing that hitting this stranger had been a bad mistake.

'Shouldn't I, now?' Rostam bellowed. 'And are you going to stop me?'

'No,' squeaked the man.

Rostam gave a snort of disgust and threw the man to the ground. 'Run away, and be careful who you're hitting next time!'

The servant did as he was told and rushed across the fields, screaming for his master.

'I suppose we're going to have trouble now, Rakhsh,' Rostam said, nudging the horse. 'Because of your greed, too! I hope you're happy.'

Rakhsh glanced up, golden stalks poking from his mouth.

Just as Rostam expected, a man he assumed was the owner of the field came galloping towards him with half a dozen warriors in tow. The owner sat on a fine horse, plated in glistening armour. *Hmmm, this man's more concerned with his appearance than his ability to fight,* Rostam thought, looking at the man's perfectly trimmed beard and his immaculately polished armour. The men behind him looked a little tougher; one had an eye-patch, and they all bore scars that told of battle. Each carried a shield and a curved sword.

'What do you mean by destroying my crops?' the landowner called, when he had drawn near enough.

'I apologize,' Rostam said. 'I have travelled far and my horse was hungry. What do you mean by telling your servant to beat anyone he finds wandering in your lands?'

'I don't like your tone, sir,' the landlord said. 'Identify yourself!'

'I am Rostam, son of Zal, and you better let me pass or there'll be trouble!'

'I am Olad, owner of all the lands you can see around you, and nobody passes through my estates without my permission. Prepare to fight!'

Rostam grinned and drew his sword, leaping on to Rakhsh's back in one bound. 'I'm always ready.'

Rakhsh gave a grunt and looked back at Rostam as if to say, *A bit of warning next time, please!*

Olad gave a nod and his six horsemen charged forward. Rostam stood his ground, waiting for them to come to him, his sword glistening in the sunlight. As the first two came close, he swung his sword back and forth, sending the men flying from their horses. 'I told you there'd be trouble!' Rostam yelled.

The second two slashed with their blades, but Rostam parried with his own sword, shattering their weapons into tiny pieces. One punched at him with his shield but Rostam just grabbed it and lifted the man out of his saddle. He swung the man above his head and sent him crashing into his comrade.

The remaining soldiers slowed down and glanced at each other warily. 'Come on!' Rostam yelled, laughing. 'I'm just getting started!'

Gritting their teeth, the two men charged forward. Rakhsh reared up, high above them, knocking one man out with his front hooves while Rostam brought his sword down on the last warrior.

Olad had dropped his spear and sat quivering on his horse. Rostam and Rakhsh sauntered over to him. Olad fumbled for his sword, getting it caught in its scabbard. Drawing alongside the fancily clad lord, Rostam extended his arm, flicking Olad on the nose. Olad flew from his saddle and landed with a crunch on the ground.

'Please don't kill me,' Olad begged. 'I have heard rumours of your mission, but you must be lost or else you wouldn't be here. If you let me live, I will tell you which way to go.'

Rostam jumped down from Rakhsh and squatted next to Olad. 'Better than that,' Rostam said. 'You are going to take me to Mazanderan.'

11. Arzhang

Olad quivered in Rostam's shadow. 'M–Mazanderan?' he stammered. 'But that is many, many miles from here. There is a great mountain range to cross, full of wild animals and strange unmentionable beasts. We will surely die!'

Rostam looked down on the quivering prince. 'I am Rostam,' he said. 'I have slain lions and serpents, warriors and enchanters! You think I fear a mountain and a few more monsters?'

Olad shrugged. 'Not really,' he said, 'but I do!'

'If you lead me to Mazanderan, I will free you,' Rostam said, laughing. 'Why, if I rescue King Kavus, he will be so grateful, he'll probably let you rule Mazanderan for him!'

Olad licked his lips. 'Really?' Rostam could see him thinking. Finally, Olad nodded. 'Very well,' he said. 'I will lead you to Mazanderan.'

Frowning, Rostam helped Olad up from the ground. 'You will follow behind me on foot. If you try to escape, Rakhsh will run you down like a deer and crush you with his iron hooves.'

Rakhsh snorted and Olad jumped away from the horse in fear. 'I won't try to escape, I promise!'

They travelled night and day. Olad stumbled behind, tethered to Rostam's saddle. Sometimes, Rostam wanted to move faster and so he flung Olad over Rakhsh's rump like an old saddlebag and they trotted on.

The mountains grew dark and cold as they climbed higher. Rostam pulled his furs close around his neck and hot breath plumed from Rakhsh's flaring nostrils. At night, they heard howling in the distance and saw strange dark shapes creeping past, but nothing leaped out at them.

Finally, Rostam looked out over a green and fertile plain. A wide river curved its way across the land.

'This is Mazanderan,' Olad said. He pointed to a large cluster of tents. 'That is the camp of Arzhang, the White Devourer's second in command. He controls the armies that protect Mazanderan. Beyond that,' – he gestured to a white-walled city – 'is the place where King Kavus is held. If you defeat Arzhang, his men will lose heart and flee. The White City will surrender to you and you can free Kavus.'

'You have stuck to your word, Olad,' Rostam said, tying Olad to a tree. 'If all you say is true, I will come back and free you.'

'Arzhang is a monster,' Olad said. 'Some say he is part wolf. What if you don't come back?'

Rostam shrugged. 'Then you'll be there for a long time, my friend.' He leaped on to Rakhsh and galloped down towards the camp.

The wind sang in his ears and Rakhsh's hooves provided a drumbeat. Rostam drew his sword as the tents of the camp drew closer. With a roar, he plunged into the camp, sending men sprawling into their campfires and bringing the tents billowing to the ground. The men were big and hairy; some of them had long yellow fangs and grey skin. They leaped at him, slashing with their claws – but each time he batted them away with his sword or sent them screaming to the floor. Rakhsh kicked and bit at the attackers, scattering as many of the monsters as his master.

Finally, the remaining assailants backed away. Rostam and Rakhsh watched as, towering above their heads, a giant waded towards them. Arzhang stood head and shoulders above Rostam himself. The blistered skin that covered his hairy body rippled with muscles and his head seemed to sprout straight from his chest. Two sharp tusks poked from Arzhang's slavering mouth and red eyes glowered at the hero. Arzhang dragged a club the size of a small tree, all studded with nails and twisted metal.

'Who dares attack our camp?' he bellowed.

Rostam leaped down from Rakhsh. 'I, Rostam, son of Zal!' he roared back. 'I have come for my King and will not rest until he is freed from your dungeons!'

Arzhang broke into the ring of warriors and slammed his club into the bare earth. 'Then prepare to die, Rostam.'

The crowd roared as Rostam ran forward, while Rakhsh galloped madly around the circle, kicking and biting to ensure none of Arzhang's soldiers tried to help. They fell back, creating an arena for the two giants to fight in.

Arzhang swung his club and Rostam had to bend over backwards to avoid the blow. The heavy wooden club whooshed close to his face, but he threw himself forward and retaliated with his sword. Monster and man struggled with each other, Arzhang swinging his club and Rostam dodging it. Finally, just as Arzhang crashed towards Rostam with his club raised, Rostam leaped forward and grabbed his enemy around the waist, bringing him to the ground with a mighty thump. Dazed by the fall, Arzhang lay still for a moment, giving Rostam a chance to raise his reddened sword.

With one lunge, Rostam finished the fight.

Then, growling, he turned to face the soldiers. A few lurched forward, thinking they could still save their leader, but Rakhsh reared up, his hooves lashing the air and they backed away again. The remaining warriors stood still, staring at Rostam and at their fallen general. An eerie silence fell over the camp. Rostam grinned and reared up to his full height.

'BOO!' he said, and it was enough for the camp to fall into chaos. The now-leaderless warriors stumbled over each other in their haste to get away. Glowing embers from the campfires were kicked over the already-fallen tents, igniting them. Soon the whole camp was a mass of flames and smoke. People fell and fought to escape in the confusion.

Rostam stroked Rakhsh's nose. 'Let's go and rescue the King,' he said.

True to his word, Rostam untied Olad from the tree and brought him down to the White City where King Kavus was held prisoner. Freeing the King would be easy now, but there was one final challenge Rostam had to face — and it was probably his deadliest.

12. The King in Chains

The huge wooden gates of the White City stood closed to Rostam and Rakhsh, but the captain of the guard realized that to get this far, they must have slain the giant Arzhang. All along the walls, the men began to mutter and talk amongst themselves. These weren't Arzhang's twisted, monster warriors; these were ordinary men, just citizens of the city, with jobs and families. Why would they want to risk their lives against a giant like Rostam? The worried murmur took over the whole city. Finally, the huge gates swung open and the captain rode out.

'We surrender,' he said. 'I will lead you to your King.'

Rostam rode behind the captain through narrow, cobbled streets. Shutters barred the windows, but every now and then a curious citizen would peek out through a crack. A few people slunk into the shadows when Rostam and the captain approached. The buildings grew tall on each side of them, whitewashed and well-kept.

The captain looked back at Rostam. 'The people fear you,' he said. 'They think you will burn their city in revenge for capturing your King and his army.'

'My King is merciful,' Rostam said. 'He may spare your city.'

King Kavus was chained in a prison cell but wept with joy when he heard Rostam's voice. The mighty warrior gave an embarrassed cough. 'My lord, I have come to take you home.'

The King sighed. 'Look at me, Rostam,' he said. 'I am blind still. The White Devourer's poisonous mist still infects me. My army is in the same condition, lying in a dark prison beneath the city.'

Olad bowed deeply. 'My lord, it is said that only the blood of the White Devourer can heal the damage done by his poison.' He glanced at Rostam. 'But I fear there is none who can defeat such a creature.'

'You think I can't beat that monster?' Rostam snorted. He knelt before the King. 'Your Highness, I will bring back the blood of the White Devourer and your sight shall be restored!'

King Kavus nodded, tears still streaming down his cheeks. 'You are truly loyal, Rostam. I don't deserve such a subject.'

Rostam bowed and turned to Olad. 'This monster must have a weakness. Think, Olad. How can I defeat this White Devourer?'

Olad stroked his beard. 'His kind are creatures of the night, and so they are weakest when the sun is highest in the sky. The Devourer lives in a cave in the distant mountains. He is guarded by forty monstrous warriors. Defeat them and bring him out into the sun, and you may have a chance.'

Rostam narrowed his eyes at Olad. 'You will come with me so I can be sure you're not lying,' he said.

Olad's face paled. 'But you promised I would be free,' he said, his voice quavering. 'I've kept my word.'

Rostam drew him aside. 'I need you to guide me, and besides,' he added, 'when you return with the White Devourer's blood, you too will be a hero in the King's newly healed eyes … ' Rostam winked.

Olad's mouth flapped open and closed, but no words came out. Rostam could see him trying to decide. 'Very well,' Olad said at last.

'Anyone would think you had a choice,' Rostam said, grinning at him.

Without further delay, Rostam, Rakhsh and Olad set off towards the distant mountains. Farmhouse doors slammed shut as they approached. Children were dragged inside as they passed through villages, and out in the fields Rostam saw shepherds hiding in trees or behind bushes.

'News of your victory over Arzhang has spread fast,' Olad said. 'Nobody dares to try and stop us or question where we are going.'

The mountains drew nearer, and soon they were climbing up into the rocky hills where pines swayed above them. Olad led them higher, up a rocky track that became narrower and narrower. Rostam glanced down to his left at the dizzying drop. 'Put one foot wrong, Rakhsh, and you'll be wishing you had wings,' he muttered.

Rakhsh considered stopping and giving himself a good shake, just to frighten Rostam, but he didn't think his master would be amused. Besides, Rakhsh wasn't too keen on heights either.

The path ended at a huge cave mouth that gaped in the mountainside. 'This is it,' Olad whispered to Rostam. 'The guards are sleeping to avoid the midday sun. Now is the time to strike, but you must be stealthy.'

Rostam strode into the clearing, raising his sword. 'White Devourer! I am Rostam, and I have come to destroy you!'

Olad looked at Rakhsh and sighed. 'Doesn't your master do "stealthy"?' he said.

Rakhsh snorted and shook his head.

A hissing noise echoed around the mouth of the cave and Rostam stood alert as dark figures came lumbering out of the shadows. They looked like men, but with horns and fangs and green, slimy skin. Strange symbols glowed red on their black armour.

The creatures began marching out, blinking in the bright sunlight, their long spears extended. Rostam's roar startled them, and he cut their spears in half with one swing of his sword. More of the guards came charging from the cave mouth, faster now, and Rostam swung his sword back and forth, cutting the creatures down.

Rostam toppled ten guards, but yet more appeared. Two managed to get behind Rostam but Rakhsh leaped from his hiding place. He bucked and kicked, sending the guards sprawling across the rocky clearing and plummeting down to the depths below.

Soon, Rostam and Rakhsh had vanquished all the guards. 'And now,' said Rostam, 'the White Devourer himself ... '

13. The White Devourer

Darkness filled the cave, but Rostam could make out a deeper darkness in the corner. As his eyes became accustomed to the cavern, he could see the Devourer's shaggy white hair and iron armour. Its body filled the back of the cave, and it rose up slowly, towering over Rostam. Two red eyes glowed at him in the dark, and pale ivory tusks poked from its mouth.

'You come to challenge me, Rostam, son of Zal?' the Devourer said, its voice shaking the walls of the cave.

'What hope do you have against one as powerful as I?'

For the first time in his life, Rostam felt real fear. This creature was bigger than any war elephant, and stronger, too. It had a quickness and cleverness about it that Rostam had never faced before. Rostam suddenly realized that the Devourer could very possibly defeat him. He thought about Rakhsh, and the times he'd told his friend off, and wished he could give him one last pat on the nose.

'I will destroy you for what you did to King Kavus,' Rostam said. 'Even if it kills me.'

The Devourer threw itself at Rostam, smashing him to the ground. Rostam felt the Devourer's hands crushing the life out of him and swung with his sword. There was little room to move, and the blow wasn't his strongest, but his blade caught the Devourer's thigh, forcing him back.

Sweat poured from Rostam's brow as he dodged the Devourer's mighty blows. Sometimes, the monster would vanish into the shadows, leaving Rostam lunging at thin air. Then it would burst from nowhere, sending Rostam flying with its huge fists. Every time the Devourer knocked him down, Rostam would stagger to his feet again and swing his sword at it. Rostam could see its powerful muscles rippling under the pale, matted hair. The darkness of the cave seemed to feed the Devourer, giving it power as quickly as the battle exhausted Rostam.

I must force it out into the light, Rostam thought. *It's my only chance to defeat it.*

The Devourer's claws slashed at him again but Rostam managed to leap aside, inching back towards the cave entrance. The Devourer laughed, and Rostam shuddered at the sight of the sharp yellow teeth that lined its mouth in jagged rows. The cave entrance grew nearer, but it wasn't close enough yet. Then the Devourer grasped Rostam's ankle, pulling him away from the light.

'You are running in fear, little human. Soon you shall die.'

Rostam swung his fist and connected with the monster's square, bristly jaw. The Devourer's head

snapped back and for a second it looked dazed. Rostam broke free and scrambled to the cave entrance. Enraged by the sudden blow, the Devourer roared and leaped after him. Rostam jabbed at the monster with his sword, increasing its fury. Again, its huge fist closed in on Rostam's ankle, but, this time, Rostam gathered his remaining strength and grabbed the creature's wrist.

With a yelp of alarm, the Devourer tried to pull away, but Rostam gritted his teeth and held on, dragging the Devourer towards the light. The cave mouth grew bigger as they neared it, and the light grew stronger. The Devourer's blows weakened as it tried to escape to the darkness at the back of the cave. Rostam saw fear in the creature's eyes, and this gave him the boost he needed. With a roar of defiance, he hurled himself backwards, still gripping the monster's wrist. They fell into the clearing in front of the cave, bathed in brilliant, searing sunlight.

The Devourer squinted, searching for Rostam in the bright sunshine, and swung its fists. Rostam dodged with ease and returned the blow, sending the Devourer staggering further away from the cave. It lashed out, blindly, the daylight sapping its powers. Rostam lunged forward with his sword and delivered a final blow. The Devourer fell to the ground, dead.

Olad leaped up from behind the rocks and bushes. 'We did it!' he yelled, punching the air.

'Let's go home,' Rostam said, collapsing on the ground.

They rode home with the Devourer's heart in a sack. Rostam dozed as he sat on Rakhsh, hardly listening to Olad.

'We're champions,' Olad said, beating his chest. 'We have defeated the White Devourer. The blood from his heart will restore King Kavus's and his soldiers' sight. Men will compose poems and songs in our honour!'

Rostam grinned and slumped in his saddle.

When they finally reached the gates of the White City, the captain and his guard stared ashen-faced at him. 'You killed the White Devourer?' the captain gasped.

'Of course we did,' Olad said, pushing him aside. 'Now make way. Rostam and Olad have to see the King.'

The captain had moved King Kavus to the royal chambers where the King of Mazanderan always stayed when he visited. Rostam took the White Devourer's heart and trickled blood over the King's eyes. Almost at once, the King opened his eyes wide, blinked several times and shook his head.

King Kavus immediately sent a servant out with a supply of the White Devourer's blood, and, before long, a distant cheer rang out across the city as the Devourer's poisonous blindness fell from Kavus's army, too.

'Rostam, I am forever in your debt. How can I ever repay you?'

Rostam bowed. 'I live to serve,' he said. 'I would beg your mercy for the people of this city. They were under the command of the King of Mazanderan ... '

King Kavus frowned. 'I will show mercy to the people,' he said, 'but not to the King. We must settle our differences. My army is no longer blind. In two days, we will be ready for battle.'

'My lord, the King of Mazanderan hid behind the White Devourer,' Rostam said. 'But now that the White Devourer is dead, the King is weak. You need not fight him – he will obey you.'

Kavus thought about this for a while. 'Very well,' he said at last. 'When you have rested and eaten, take a letter to the King. He will pay a tribute to us for imprisoning us and treating us so badly.'

Rostam bowed and left the King's chamber.

Olad ran after him. His face boiled crimson. 'What are you doing? What about my reward?'

'Be patient!' Rostam said, turning on Olad so quickly it made him jump. 'You will see what happens next!'

14. The Stone King

The journey to the King of Mazanderan's palace didn't take long, and soon Rakhsh was standing in the royal stables eating the finest oats while Olad waited with him, grumbling about being treated like a stable hand.

Rostam strode into the throne room with a cold heart. This King was a cruel and wicked man who used enchantments to get his way. It was time for him to give up the throne.

Rich tapestries hung along the walls of the throne room, and courtiers wearing silks and jewels huddled in corners muttering and pointing at Rostam. The King sat in the

centre, in a huge throne. It was carved and painted to resemble peacock feathers, and plump cushions supported the King's back.

The King himself looked wizened and old. His long grey beard wriggled down his chest, obscuring his rich purple robe. The golden crown wobbled on his head and the rings of office seemed to hang off his skinny fingers. His eyes flickered around the room as Rostam approached.

'Speak, messenger of Kavus. What does your craven ruler want?'

Rostam gritted his teeth at the insult. 'His Highness King Kavus bids you greetings and orders me to present this letter,' he said, handing over a scroll.

The paper trembled in the King's hand as he read. 'How dare he?' the King muttered. 'He invades my land and then demands compensation when he is defeated? The arrogance of the man!'

'My lord feels that in the battle you had help that was not entirely of this earth,' Rostam said, narrowing his eyes at the King. 'He says that without the White Devourer, your armies wouldn't have stood a chance against him.'

'I know what he thinks!' the King snapped. 'And I know who you are, Rostam, son of Zal! Tell me that your King doesn't hide behind you!'

Rostam smiled and bowed. 'I think you are mistaken, my lord. I am not Rostam. I am just a humble servant. Rostam is much stronger than me!'

An alarmed murmur ran around the throne room and Rostam smirked. If the generals and dukes here thought that all of Kavus's men were as big and strong as Rostam, they would approach a battle with fear in their hearts.

'Enough!' the King yelled, stamping his foot. 'Tell your master to gather his puny forces and be ready to meet my army in two days' time. We will soon find out who is the strongest.'

Rostam bowed and left the throne room. Olad waited for him at the stables. 'Well?' he said. 'What now?'

Rostam's eyes glowed. 'War,' he said, 'and then you will receive your reward!'

* * *

The King of Mazanderan's men stood in disciplined lines at dawn two days later. Their flags fluttered in the breeze and the sun shone on their armour. Olad peered from the walls of the White City and shivered. 'I've never seen an army before,' he said. 'There are so many of them; how can we ever win?'

Rostam laughed. 'If you could see them clearly, you'd know they are trembling with fear,' he said. 'Most of them will run when we open the gates.' He hurried down from the walls and climbed on Rakhsh.

King Kavus and his army were gathered on horseback at the gate. Now they could see again, the soldiers were ready to take revenge on the King who had blinded them. The captain of the city had joined them, along with his soldiers. 'Our King would punish us harshly for having let you out of prison,' he said, simply. 'We have no choice.'

Rostam raised his sword at the head of the column. 'These men are soft!' he bellowed. 'These men let wicked creatures do their fighting for them! These men fear us!'

The soldiers behind Rostam roared, and when the gates opened they charged towards the enemy like lions after prey. Rostam felt the wind filling his ears and Rakhsh's hooves thundering beneath him. The Mazanderani army let up a feeble roar and, as Rostam had suspected, half of them turned and began to head away from the battle. The other half charged forward.

Grunts and screams filled the air and metal clashed on metal as swords clanged together. Men fell and arrows flew. Rostam swung with his sword, knocking men to the ground and barging them with his shield. All around him King Kavus's men fought bravely, and soon the Mazanderani troops began to fall back.

Roaring like a lion, Rostam forced his way through the crush of men until he found the King of Mazanderan's chariot. The old man's eyes widened in alarm as Rostam cut through his bodyguards and stood before him. 'Now, old man,' Rostam bellowed, 'do you surrender?'

The King of Mazanderan gave a wily grin and twisted the ring on his index finger. A grey mist surrounded him and then solidified, transforming him into a huge boulder. All around Rostam, the battle halted as the Mazanderani warriors realized that their King had vanished. Some soldiers ran; others dropped their swords and stood with their hands open in surrender.

Rostam was still staring at the boulder as King Kavus approached. 'What enchantment is this?' the King snarled. 'The King of Mazanderan has turned himself into a stone?'

'He has, my lord, but I think I have the solution,' Rostam said, wrapping his mighty arms around the boulder and lifting it. The curious King, and soldiers from both sides, forgot their battle and followed Rostam as he carried the stone back to the city, through the gates and up to the walls.

Olad joined them. 'My King, why is Rostam carrying a huge boulder up the steps?' he said. 'Hasn't he proved himself enough? He's always showing off!'

Kavus smiled. 'Watch, Olad,' he said.

Rostam's muscles bulged as he struggled up each step, sweat running down his face and back. When he finally reached the top of the walls, he balanced the rock on top of the parapet.

'This is your only chance,' Rostam said. 'Change back into the King, or I will smash you into a thousand pieces on the rocky floor below.' The rock remained still and didn't change. 'I'm going to count to three and then I'll push you over.'

The stone began to shimmer and become misty. The King appeared, standing on the battlements with a gleaming dagger. He lunged at Kavus, but Rostam was quicker. With a hard shove, Rostam sent the King of Mazanderan tumbling over the edge and down to the rocks below.

The streets erupted with cheers.

'It seems that the Mazanderani didn't really like being ruled by wicked creatures and enchanters,' King Kavus said, placing a hand on Rostam's shoulder. 'Rostam, name your reward. You have done me a greater service than any king deserves.'

Rostam glanced over at Olad. 'Well, it seems to me, my lord, that you will need someone to rule your new country for you and make sure your law is obeyed. Olad left his estates over the mountains to help me rescue you. He didn't flinch when I asked him to risk life and limb to destroy the White Devourer. I think he would make an excellent steward, ruling in your absence.'

Kavus looked Olad up and down and then clapped him on the shoulder. 'Very well!' he said. 'I appoint you as Steward of Mazanderan. Rule wisely, Olad!'

Olad bowed deeply, clearly not able to believe his luck. 'I will, my lord, I will!'

For a short while King Kavus acted humbly and wisely. He remembered how his greed had led him to blindness. Sadly, however, Kavus had a short memory and a high opinion of himself, and so his humility didn't last long.

15. King of the Skies

Even though the White Devourer was dead, many of his followers remained scattered across the land, causing mischief and trouble wherever they could. One such creature hid in the woods and waited for King Kavus to pass on his way home from Mazanderan. As the King rode past, this creature made himself look like a simple peasant and stumbled out in front of the King's party.

At once, one of the King's guard grabbed him and put a sword to his throat. 'What do you mean by startling the King so?' he demanded.

'Forgive me, Your Worship!' the peasant begged, showing the guard a bunch of wild flowers. 'I merely wanted to give the great King a gift and ask him a question.'

'Be off with you,' the guard said, cuffing the peasant with his gloved hand.

Kavus waved the guard away. 'Let the man speak,' he said. 'He cannot harm me with words, and if he offends me, you can deal with him.'

The guard bowed and shoved the peasant forward roughly.

'Forgive me, sire,' the peasant said again, 'I am just a simple peasant and I don't understand the ways of the world like you do. I dig soil while you feast and read and listen to fine music. You rule the deserts and the forests, the mountains and the sea ... '

'Get on with it,' Kavus said, smiling at the compliments.

'I'm sorry, sire,' the peasant said. 'All animals on the land are yours and all fish in the sea. But I wonder ... '

'What?' Kavus snapped. 'What?'

'Who rules the skies? Is it the eagle or the moon?' the peasant asked, looking puzzled. 'If a man dares question you in far-off Egypt, you can go and punish him, but even you cannot go up into the skies ... '

Kavus reddened and waved a dismissive hand at the man. 'Nonsense,' he muttered. 'Talk sense. Who can fly?'

The peasant shrugged and bowed his head again. 'I know nothing, sire, but I believe that if you rule the land, you should rule the skies, too.'

'My lord,' a guard said. 'The man is clearly not talking sense. Should I get rid of him for you?'

Kavus laughed. 'No, let him go,' he said. 'He's done no harm – and in fact, he's made me think.'

The peasant bowed and retreated into the bushes from where he came. Nobody saw the smirk of victory on his face.

Kavus rode on, but he was quiet and thoughtful all the way home. The peasant's idea had wormed its way into his head. *Why should I be bound by the earth? I'm King Kavus, ruler of all. He's right: I should be able to fly and discover the secrets of the skies.*

Weeks passed and Kavus could think of nothing else. *The moon and stars laugh at me,* he thought as he went to bed. *The sun should bow to me,* he thought as he rose in the morning.

Finally, he found a wise man who claimed to be able to make him fly. The ragged old man seemed as fanciful as the peasant to Kavus's advisors, but Kavus treated him like a visionary.

'First, you need four eagles,' the man said, picking lice from his sackcloth tunic. 'The biggest and strongest you can find!'

Kavus made a declaration and the people of his kingdom hurried to the mountains to find the biggest and strongest birds they could. Many perished: they fell from cliffs or were attacked by birds protecting their nests. But at last Kavus had four of the biggest and most powerful birds ever seen.

'Now,' said the old man, scratching his thin white hair, 'have your carpenters build a chair with four tall poles at each corner. Make it strong but as light as possible.'

The King's carpenters hammered and sawed until they had created a chair of the lightest wood. Kavus settled himself on to the chair. It felt just perfect. Soon he would discover the secrets of the heavens and rule the skies!

The old man gave a yellow-toothed grin and clapped his hands. 'You tie your eagles to the bottom of each leg of the chair,' he said, 'and you fix a juicy piece of meat to the top of each pole on the corner. Be sure you are sitting comfortably, though!'

The King called for his eagles and his cook, and had the chair placed in his garden. 'Tie the eagles to the legs!' he ordered, climbing on to the chair.

The cook arrived with four of the hugest, juiciest steaks imaginable and nailed them to the top of the poles. The meat was so heavy, it almost unbalanced his ladder.

'Now, release the eagles!' the old man shrieked and he fell about cackling as the eagles smelled the meat and began flapping their wings. As they flew up, straining to get at the meat, the chair lifted. It tilted and wobbled at first, but soon Kavus got his balance right and slowly the chair drifted up. The King looked down and frowned; the figures below him were shrinking by the second as he flew up, but he was sure the old man had changed. His skin looked grey and was now covered in boils. Gnarled horns sprang from his head as he laughed and pointed with a long, crooked finger.

'I think I've been fooled again,' King Kavus muttered, but he couldn't think what to do.

Higher and higher he went. The palace became a tiny dot in the green and brown landscape. For a while, he forgot his fears and marvelled at the view. He could see the distant mountains, the lakes and even the sea. Then clouds closed around him and it became colder. He shivered.

Still the eagles flapped, desperate to get at the meat. A stiff wind began to blow, chilling Kavus even more and pushing him along as well as up. 'Help!' he yelled, and tried to kick out at the eagles.

The chair bucked, nearly tipping him out into the open sky. Kavus sat back and gripped the sides.

16. A Magical Feather

The flapping of the eagles' wings grew slower, as gradually they tired and gave up trying to get the meat. Now all they wanted to do was to escape from the ropes that tied them to the chair. Kavus yelped as they flew in all directions, making the chair twist and flip like a horse with a bramble under its saddle. Somehow, he managed to maintain his grip, and slowly the eagles ran out of energy. The chair began to fall faster, the wind whistling in Kavus's ears.

'Help!' he yelled. The eagles, seeing the danger, flapped once more, slowing the descent but not halting it. They were exhausted and their chests pumped in and out as they tried to catch breath and fly. The chair fell again and the clouds broke. Kavus screamed as he saw the hard green earth coming back into focus. Nearer and nearer it came, rising up to meet him.

Kavus squeezed his eyes shut. 'Please, please, please, save me from this and I'll never be so big-headed again,' he muttered under his breath.

The eagles made one final try at flapping and the chair slowed just as Kavus could begin to make out the individual spines on the thorn bushes beneath them. One of the strings snapped, and then another. The two free eagles flew up and grabbed the meat, gripping it tight as they tried to rip it from the poles. The chair slowed again. Jealous of their companions, the remaining eagles pecked at their bindings and broke free. The chair tipped forward, sending Kavus hurtling down into the nearest thorn bush. His skin burned as he fell through the branches, and all went black.

* * *

Rostam could tell by the look on Zal's face that he had bad news as he walked across to the stables. Just like the last time Zal had brought him news about the King, Rostam was brushing Rakhsh's flanks to a brilliant shine. 'Is it King Kavus again?' Rostam asked as Zal approached.

Zal nodded. 'He's in big trouble this time. He made himself a flying chair, but it looks as though it's worked a bit too well. He took off a week ago, and no one's seen him since. Think you can help?'

'What d'you think, Rakhsh?' Rostam said, patting his neck. Rakhsh gave a long sigh and nodded his head.

With full saddlebags and waterskins, they set off to rescue the King. The sky was blue but a cold breeze played with Rakhsh's mane and made them both shiver. At last, they came upon a small troop of the King's warriors. Dust coated their armour and worry creased their faces. They waved and cheered as Rostam arrived, sure that their problems were over.

'We haven't seen the King for seven whole days, and we are worried,' their captain said. 'Please help us!'

Dismounting, Rostam pulled a feather out of his belt pouch and stared at it. This was a feather from the Simorgh – the magical creature who had raised his father Zal all those years ago. The Simorgh had entrusted Zal with a few enchanted feathers, to be used only in times of emergency. If placed in a fire, the feather would summon the Simorgh herself.

Rostam strode to the soldiers' campfire and placed the feather in the flames. A searing heat burned Rostam's fingertips, but he held on tight to the feather. Smoke boiled out of the smouldering feather and formed a cloud above them.

Slowly, the cloud solidified into the shape of a creature with the head of a fierce animal, eagle's wings and a lion's body. The soldiers backed away in fear, but Rostam bowed.

The Simorgh bowed too and smiled. 'Rostam, son of Zal, I have been watching your progress with interest,' she said. 'You need my help.'

'I do, oh great Simorgh,' Rostam confessed. 'Our ruler, King Kavus, made a flying chair and then got himself lost.' Rostam tried, but he couldn't keep the annoyance out of his voice.

'I will fly high and use my sharp eyes to locate him,' the Simorgh said. She flapped her wings and vanished high in the clouds.

A few long minutes later, she returned with a torn and bedraggled King Kavus in her claws. She dumped him at Rostam's feet.

'Rostam, this beast attacked me. Kill it now!' Kavus stammered.

The last time Rostam saw the King in such a state, he had felt embarrassed for him. Now Rostam felt anger. 'This is the Simorgh, protector of the family of Zal. I will not lift a finger to harm her,' he said. 'It is arrogance that gets you into these situations, and innocent men die. How many warriors perished on the plains of Mazanderan? I am tired of chasing after you and rescuing you!'

Kavus bowed before him. 'Forgive me, Rostam. You are right. I am an arrogant and selfish ruler. I promise I will change my ways.'

But Rostam turned his back on Kavus. 'I have had enough of you,' he said. 'Don't call on me until you are worthy to sit on the throne.'

Humph! Rakhsh snorted and sidled over to Rostam.

'Come on,' said Rostam, with a smile of satisfaction. 'We're going home, Rakhsh. Kavus can walk for all I care!'

The Simorgh flapped her mighty wings and flew above them as the hero and his faithful horse galloped away, eager to begin the many adventures that still awaited them.

I flew with Rostam and Rakhsh all the way to their home near my lofty mountains. Rostam was as good as his word and stayed away from Kavus for many years. Rostam and Rakhsh travelled to all the corners of the Empire, seeking challenge and adventure.

With each victory Rostam's pride grew, until he was almost as arrogant as Kavus himself and even considered taking the King's place. But in his heart he knew he could never do so. He may have been full of pride but he was always loyal, just like Rakhsh.

King Kavus spent a long time regretting his greed and arrogance, and learning to become a better and a wiser ruler. Eventually he did call Rostam back. Rostam answered the call and served him bravely for the rest of his days.